THIS BOOK BELONGS TO:

_____

NAME ....

GIFT IDEAS ....

BUDGET .... **ACTUAL** ....

STORE/GIFT ....

NOTES ....

☐ ORDERED!   ☐ GOT IT!

☐ WRAPPED!   ☐ DELIVERED!

NAME

GIFT IDEAS

BUDGET

ACTUAL

STORE/GIFT

NOTES

☐ ORDERED! ☐ GOT IT!

☐ WRAPPED! ☐ DELIVERED!

NAME

GIFT IDEAS

BUDGET

ACTUAL

STORE/GIFT

NOTES

☐ ORDERED!　　　　☐ GOT IT!

☐ WRAPPED!　　　　☐ DELIVERED!

NAME

GIFT IDEAS

BUDGET

ACTUAL

STORE/GIFT

NOTES

☐ ORDERED!

☐ GOT IT!

☐ WRAPPED!

☐ DELIVERED!

NAME

GIFT IDEAS

BUDGET

ACTUAL

STORE/GIFT

NOTES

☐ ORDERED! ☐ GOT IT!

☐ WRAPPED! ☐ DELIVERED!

NAME

GIFT IDEAS

BUDGET

ACTUAL

STORE/GIFT

NOTES

☐ ORDERED!   ☐ GOT IT!

☐ WRAPPED!   ☐ DELIVERED!

NAME

GIFT IDEAS

BUDGET

ACTUAL

STORE/GIFT

NOTES

☐ ORDERED!   ☐ GOT IT!

☐ WRAPPED!   ☐ DELIVERED!

NAME

GIFT IDEAS

BUDGET

ACTUAL

STORE/GIFT

NOTES

☐ ORDERED!   ☐ GOT IT!

☐ WRAPPED!   ☐ DELIVERED!

NAME

GIFT IDEAS

BUDGET

ACTUAL

STORE/GIFT

NOTES

☐ ORDERED!   ☐ GOT IT!

☐ WRAPPED!   ☐ DELIVERED!

NAME

GIFT IDEAS

BUDGET

ACTUAL

STORE/GIFT

NOTES

☐ ORDERED!   ☐ GOT IT!

☐ WRAPPED!   ☐ DELIVERED!

NAME

GIFT IDEAS

BUDGET

ACTUAL

STORE/GIFT

NOTES

☐ ORDERED!   ☐ GOT IT!

☐ WRAPPED!   ☐ DELIVERED!

NAME

GIFT IDEAS

BUDGET

ACTUAL

STORE/GIFT

NOTES

☐ ORDERED!   ☐ GOT IT!

☐ WRAPPED!   ☐ DELIVERED!

NAME

GIFT IDEAS

BUDGET

ACTUAL

STORE/GIFT

NOTES

☐ ORDERED! ☐ GOT IT!

☐ WRAPPED! ☐ DELIVERED!

NAME

GIFT IDEAS

BUDGET

ACTUAL

STORE/GIFT

NOTES

☐ ORDERED!　　　☐ GOT IT!

☐ WRAPPED!　　　☐ DELIVERED!

NAME ....

GIFT IDEAS ....

BUDGET ....   ACTUAL ....

STORE/GIFT ....

NOTES ....

☐ ORDERED!   ☐ GOT IT!

☐ WRAPPED!   ☐ DELIVERED!

NAME

GIFT IDEAS

BUDGET

ACTUAL

STORE/GIFT

NOTES

☐ ORDERED!   ☐ GOT IT!

☐ WRAPPED!   ☐ DELIVERED!

NAME

GIFT IDEAS

BUDGET

ACTUAL

STORE/GIFT

NOTES

☐ ORDERED!　　☐ GOT IT!

☐ WRAPPED!　　☐ DELIVERED!

NAME

GIFT IDEAS

BUDGET

ACTUAL

STORE/GIFT

NOTES

☐ ORDERED!   ☐ GOT IT!

☐ WRAPPED!   ☐ DELIVERED!

NAME

GIFT IDEAS

BUDGET

ACTUAL

STORE/GIFT

NOTES

☐ ORDERED!   ☐ GOT IT!

☐ WRAPPED!   ☐ DELIVERED!

NAME

GIFT IDEAS

BUDGET

ACTUAL

STORE/GIFT

NOTES

☐ ORDERED!   ☐ GOT IT!

☐ WRAPPED!   ☐ DELIVERED!

NAME

GIFT IDEAS

BUDGET

ACTUAL

STORE/GIFT

NOTES

☐ ORDERED!   ☐ GOT IT!

☐ WRAPPED!   ☐ DELIVERED!

NAME

GIFT IDEAS

BUDGET

ACTUAL

STORE/GIFT

NOTES

☐ ORDERED!   ☐ GOT IT!

☐ WRAPPED!   ☐ DELIVERED!

NAME ....

GIFT IDEAS ....

BUDGET ....   ACTUAL ....

STORE/GIFT ....

NOTES ....

☐ ORDERED!   ☐ GOT IT!

☐ WRAPPED!   ☐ DELIVERED!

NAME

GIFT IDEAS

BUDGET

ACTUAL

STORE/GIFT

NOTES

☐ ORDERED!   ☐ GOT IT!

☐ WRAPPED!   ☐ DELIVERED!

NAME

GIFT IDEAS

BUDGET

ACTUAL

STORE/GIFT

NOTES

- [ ] ORDERED!
- [ ] GOT IT!
- [ ] WRAPPED!
- [ ] DELIVERED!

NAME ....

GIFT IDEAS ....

BUDGET ....   ACTUAL ....

STORE/GIFT ....

NOTES ....

☐ ORDERED!   ☐ GOT IT!

☐ WRAPPED!   ☐ DELIVERED!

NAME

GIFT IDEAS

BUDGET

ACTUAL

STORE/GIFT

NOTES

☐ ORDERED!   ☐ GOT IT!

☐ WRAPPED!   ☐ DELIVERED!

NAME ....

GIFT IDEAS ....

BUDGET ....   ACTUAL ....

STORE/GIFT ....

NOTES ....

☐ ORDERED!   ☐ GOT IT!

☐ WRAPPED!   ☐ DELIVERED!

NAME

GIFT IDEAS

BUDGET

ACTUAL

STORE/GIFT

NOTES

☐ ORDERED! ☐ GOT IT!

☐ WRAPPED! ☐ DELIVERED!

NAME

GIFT IDEAS

BUDGET

ACTUAL

STORE/GIFT

NOTES

☐ ORDERED!   ☐ GOT IT!

☐ WRAPPED!   ☐ DELIVERED!

NAME

GIFT IDEAS

BUDGET

ACTUAL

STORE/GIFT

NOTES

☐ ORDERED!   ☐ GOT IT!

☐ WRAPPED!   ☐ DELIVERED!

NAME

GIFT IDEAS

BUDGET

ACTUAL

STORE/GIFT

NOTES

☐ ORDERED!   ☐ GOT IT!

☐ WRAPPED!   ☐ DELIVERED!

NAME

GIFT IDEAS

BUDGET

ACTUAL

STORE/GIFT

NOTES

☐ ORDERED!　　☐ GOT IT!

☐ WRAPPED!　　☐ DELIVERED!

NAME

GIFT IDEAS

BUDGET

ACTUAL

STORE/GIFT

NOTES

☐ ORDERED!   ☐ GOT IT!

☐ WRAPPED!   ☐ DELIVERED!

NAME

GIFT IDEAS

BUDGET

ACTUAL

STORE/GIFT

NOTES

☐ ORDERED!　　　☐ GOT IT!

☐ WRAPPED!　　　☐ DELIVERED!

NAME ....

GIFT IDEAS ....

BUDGET ....

ACTUAL ....

STORE/GIFT ....

NOTES ....

☐ ORDERED!   ☐ GOT IT!

☐ WRAPPED!   ☐ DELIVERED!

NAME

GIFT IDEAS

BUDGET

ACTUAL

STORE/GIFT

NOTES

☐ ORDERED!

☐ GOT IT!

☐ WRAPPED!

☐ DELIVERED!

NAME

GIFT IDEAS

BUDGET

ACTUAL

STORE/GIFT

NOTES

☐ ORDERED!   ☐ GOT IT!

☐ WRAPPED!   ☐ DELIVERED!

NAME

GIFT IDEAS

BUDGET

ACTUAL

STORE/GIFT

NOTES

☐ ORDERED!   ☐ GOT IT!

☐ WRAPPED!   ☐ DELIVERED!

NAME

GIFT IDEAS

BUDGET

ACTUAL

STORE/GIFT

NOTES

☐ ORDERED!   ☐ GOT IT!

☐ WRAPPED!   ☐ DELIVERED!

NAME

GIFT IDEAS

BUDGET

ACTUAL

STORE/GIFT

NOTES

☐ ORDERED!   ☐ GOT IT!

☐ WRAPPED!   ☐ DELIVERED!

NAME

GIFT IDEAS

BUDGET

ACTUAL

STORE/GIFT

NOTES

☐ ORDERED!   ☐ GOT IT!

☐ WRAPPED!   ☐ DELIVERED!

NAME

GIFT IDEAS

BUDGET

ACTUAL

STORE/GIFT

NOTES

☐ ORDERED! ☐ GOT IT!

☐ WRAPPED! ☐ DELIVERED!

NAME

GIFT IDEAS

BUDGET

ACTUAL

STORE/GIFT

NOTES

☐ ORDERED!   ☐ GOT IT!

☐ WRAPPED!   ☐ DELIVERED!

NAME

GIFT IDEAS

BUDGET

ACTUAL

STORE/GIFT

NOTES

☐ ORDERED!   ☐ GOT IT!

☐ WRAPPED!   ☐ DELIVERED!

NAME

GIFT IDEAS

BUDGET

ACTUAL

STORE/GIFT

NOTES

☐ ORDERED!   ☐ GOT IT!

☐ WRAPPED!   ☐ DELIVERED!

NAME

GIFT IDEAS

BUDGET

ACTUAL

STORE/GIFT

NOTES

☐ ORDERED!   ☐ GOT IT!

☐ WRAPPED!   ☐ DELIVERED!

NAME ....

GIFT IDEAS ....

BUDGET .... ACTUAL ....

STORE/GIFT ....

NOTES ....

☐ ORDERED!   ☐ GOT IT!

☐ WRAPPED!   ☐ DELIVERED!

NAME

GIFT IDEAS

BUDGET

ACTUAL

STORE/GIFT

NOTES

☐ ORDERED!   ☐ GOT IT!

☐ WRAPPED!   ☐ DELIVERED!

NAME

GIFT IDEAS

BUDGET

ACTUAL

STORE/GIFT

NOTES

☐ ORDERED!   ☐ GOT IT!

☐ WRAPPED!   ☐ DELIVERED!

NAME

GIFT IDEAS

BUDGET

ACTUAL

STORE/GIFT

NOTES

☐ ORDERED!   ☐ GOT IT!

☐ WRAPPED!   ☐ DELIVERED!

NAME

GIFT IDEAS

BUDGET

ACTUAL

STORE/GIFT

NOTES

☐ ORDERED! ☐ GOT IT!

☐ WRAPPED! ☐ DELIVERED!

NAME

GIFT IDEAS

BUDGET

ACTUAL

STORE/GIFT

NOTES

☐ ORDERED!   ☐ GOT IT!

☐ WRAPPED!   ☐ DELIVERED!

NAME

GIFT IDEAS

BUDGET

ACTUAL

STORE/GIFT

NOTES

☐ ORDERED!   ☐ GOT IT!

☐ WRAPPED!   ☐ DELIVERED!

NAME

GIFT IDEAS

BUDGET

ACTUAL

STORE/GIFT

NOTES

☐ ORDERED!   ☐ GOT IT!

☐ WRAPPED!   ☐ DELIVERED!

NAME

GIFT IDEAS

BUDGET

ACTUAL

STORE/GIFT

NOTES

☐ ORDERED!   ☐ GOT IT!

☐ WRAPPED!   ☐ DELIVERED!

NAME ....

GIFT IDEAS ....

BUDGET ....   ACTUAL ....

STORE/GIFT ....

NOTES ....

☐ ORDERED!   ☐ GOT IT!

☐ WRAPPED!   ☐ DELIVERED!

NAME

GIFT IDEAS

BUDGET

ACTUAL

STORE/GIFT

NOTES

☐ ORDERED!   ☐ GOT IT!

☐ WRAPPED!   ☐ DELIVERED!

NAME

GIFT IDEAS

BUDGET

ACTUAL

STORE/GIFT

NOTES

☐ ORDERED! ☐ GOT IT!

☐ WRAPPED! ☐ DELIVERED!

LIST OVERVIEW NAME	BUDGET	ACTUAL	ORDERED	GOT IT!	WRAPPED	DONE!

LIST OVERVIEW NAME	BUDGET	ACTUAL	ORDERED	GOT IT!	WRAPPED	

LIST OVERVIEW NAME	BUDGET	ACTUAL	ORDERED	GOT IT!	WRAPPED	DONE!

LIST OVERVIEW NAME	BUDGET	ACTUAL	ORDERED	GOT IT!	WRAPPED	

Made in the USA
San Bernardino, CA
21 November 2018